In the Year 1964

by

Kerry Butters.

In the Year 1964

Millennium: 2nd millennium

Centuries: 19th century – **20th century** – 21st century

Decades: 1930s 1940s 1950s – **1960s** – 1970s 1980s 1990s

Years: 1961 1962 1963 – **1964** – 1965 1966 1967

1964 (MCMLXIV) was a leap year starting on Wednesday (dominical letter ED) of the Gregorian calendar, the 1964th year of the Common Era (CE) and *Anno Domini* (AD) designations, the 964th year of the 2nd millennium, the 64th year of the 20th century, and the 5th year of the 1960s decade.

Contents

Events

January

January 8: U.S. President Lyndon B. Johnson's War on Poverty

1964 Winter Olympics

- January – The Federation of Rhodesia and Nyasaland is dissolved.
- January 5
  - U.S. Senator Barry Goldwater announces that he will seek the Republican nomination for President.
  - In the first meeting between leaders of the Roman Catholic and Orthodox churches since the 15th century, Pope Paul VI and Patriarch Athenagoras I of Constantinople meet in Jerusalem.
- January 7 – A British firm, the Leyland Motor Corp., announces the sale of 450 buses to the Cuban government, challenging the United States blockade of Cuba.
- January 8 – In his first State of the Union Address, U.S. President Lyndon Johnson declares a "War on Poverty".
- January 9 – *Martyrs' Day*: Armed clashes between United States troops and Panamanian civilians in the Panama Canal Zone precipitate a major international crisis, resulting in the deaths of 21 Panamanians and 4 U.S. soldiers.
- January 10 – *Introducing... The Beatles* is released by Chicago's Vee-Jay Records to get the jump on Capitol Records' release of *Meet the Beatles!*, scheduled for January 20. The two record companies fight over Vee-Jay's release of this album in court.
- January 11 – United States Surgeon General Luther Terry reports that smoking may be hazardous to one's health (the first such statement from the U.S. government).
- January 12
  - Zanzibar Revolution: The predominantly Arab government of Zanzibar is overthrown by African nationalist rebels; a United States Navy destroyer evacuates 61 U.S. citizens.

- Routine U.S. naval patrols of the South China Sea begin.
- January 13 – In Manchester, New Hampshire, 14-year-old Pamela Mason is murdered. Edward Coolidge is tried and convicted of the crime, but the conviction is set aside by the landmark Fourth Amendment case "Coolidge vs. New Hampshire (1971)."
- January 16
  - Musical *Hello, Dolly!* opens in New York's St. James Theatre.
  - John Glenn, the first American to orbit the Earth, resigns from NASA.
- January 17 – John Glenn announces that he will seek the Democratic nomination for U.S. Senator from Ohio.
- January 18 – Plans to build the New York City World Trade Center are announced.
- January 20 – *Meet the Beatles!*, the first Beatles album from Capitol Records in the United States, is released ten days after Chicago's Vee-Jay Records releases *Introducing... The Beatles*. The two record companies battle it out in court for months, eventually coming to a conclusion.
- January 22 – Kenneth Kaunda is inaugurated as the first Prime Minister of Northern Rhodesia.
- January 23
  - Pope Paul VI institutes the World Day of Prayer for Vocations. During this celebration the Pope reminds the universal Church that still today salvation comes to everyone. It continues to be celebrated every Fourth Sunday of Easter also known as Good Shepherd Sunday.

- Thirteen years after its proposal and nearly 2 years after its passage by the United States Senate, the 24th Amendment to the United States Constitution, prohibiting the use of poll taxes in national elections, is ratified.
- Arthur Miller's *After the Fall* opens Off-Broadway. A semi-autobiographical work, it arouses controversy over his portrayal of late ex-wife Marilyn Monroe.
- January 27
  - France and the People's Republic of China announce their decision to establish diplomatic relations.
  - U.S. Senator Margaret Chase Smith, 66, announces her candidacy for the Republican presidential nomination.
- January 28 – A U.S. Air Force jet training plane that strays into East Germany is shot down by Soviet fighters near Erfurt; all 3 crew men are killed.
- January 29–February 9 – The 1964 Winter Olympics are held in Innsbruck, Austria.
- January 29
  - The Soviet Union launches 2 scientific satellites, Elektron I and II, from a single rocket.
  - Ranger 6 is launched by NASA, on a mission to carry television cameras and crash-land on the Moon.
- January 30 – General Nguyễn Khánh leads a bloodless military coup d'état, replacing Dương Văn Minh as Prime Minister of South Vietnam.

February

- February 1 – The Beatles vault to the #1 spot on the U.S. singles charts for the first time, with "I Want to Hold Your Hand", starting the British Invasion in America.
- February 3 – Protesting against alleged de facto school racial segregation, Black and Puerto Rican groups in New York City boycott public schools.
- February 4
  - The Government of the United States authorizes the Twenty-fourth Amendment to the United States Constitution, outlawing the poll tax.
- February 5 – India backs out of its promise to hold a plebiscite in the disputed territory of Kashmir. In 1948, India had taken the issue of Kashmir to the United Nations Security Council and offered to hold a plebiscite in the held Kashmir under UN supervision.
- February 6 – Cuba cuts off the normal water supply to the United States Guantanamo Bay Naval Base, in reprisal for the U.S. seizure 4 days earlier of 4 Cuban fishing boats off the coast of Florida.
- February 7
  - A Jackson, Mississippi jury, trying Byron De La Beckwith for the murder of Medgar Evers in June 1963, reports that it cannot reach a verdict, resulting in a mistrial.
  - The Beatles arrive from England at New York City's JFK International Airport, receiving a tumultuous

reception from a throng of screaming fans, marking the first occurrence of "Beatlemania" in the United States.

- February 9 – The Beatles appear on *The Ed Sullivan Show*, marking their first live performance on American television. Seen by an estimated 73 million viewers, the appearance becomes the catalyst for the mid-1960s "British Invasion" of American popular music.
- February 11
    - Greeks and Turks begin fighting in Limassol, Cyprus.
    - The Republic of China (Taiwan) severs diplomatic relations with France because of French recognition of the People's Republic of China.
- February 17
    - *Wesberry v. Sanders* (376 US 1 1964): The Supreme Court of the United States rules that congressional districts have to be approximately equal in population.
    - Gabonese president Léon M'ba is toppled by a military coup and his archrival, Jean-Hilaire Aubame, is installed in his place. However, French intervention restores M'ba's government the next day.
- February 23 – Chrysler's second generation hemi racing engine debuts at the Daytona 500. The 426 hemi-powered Plymouth of Richard Petty (#43) wins. Hemi-powered Plymouths finish 1-2-3.
- February 25 – Cassius Clay (later Muhammad Ali) beats Sonny Liston in Miami Beach, Florida, and is crowned the heavyweight champion of the world.
- February 26 – U.S. politician John Glenn slips on a bathroom rug in his Columbus, Ohio apartment and hits his head on the bathtub, injuring his left inner ear, and prompting him

(later that week) to withdraw from the race for the Democratic Party Senate nomination.

- February 27 – The government of Italy asks for help to keep the Leaning Tower of Pisa from toppling over.
- February 29 – U.S. President Lyndon B. Johnson announces that the United States has developed a jet airplane (the A-11), capable of sustained flight at more than 2,000 miles per hour (3,200 km/h) and of altitudes of more than 70,000 feet (21,000 m).

March

- March 4 – Teamsters President Jimmy Hoffa is convicted by a federal jury of tampering with a federal jury in 1962.
- March 6
  - Constantine II becomes King of Greece, upon the death of his father King Paul.
  - Malcolm X, suspended from the Nation of Islam, says in New York City that he is forming a black nationalist party.
- March 9
  - *New York Times Co. v Sullivan* (376 US 254 1964): The United States Supreme Court rules that under the First Amendment, speech criticizing political figures cannot be censored.
  - The first Ford Mustang rolls off the assembly line at Ford Motor Company.

- March 10
  - Soviet military forces shoot down an unarmed reconnaissance bomber that had strayed into East Germany; the 3 U.S. flyers parachute to safety.
  - Henry Cabot Lodge Jr., Ambassador to South Vietnam, wins the New Hampshire Republican primary.
- March 12 – Malcolm X leaves the Nation of Islam.
- March 13 – *The New York Times* misreports that 38 neighbors of Kitty Genovese, 28, fail to respond to her cries, as she is being stabbed to death in Queens, New York City, prompting investigation into the bystander effect.
- March 14 – A Dallas, Texas jury finds Jack Ruby guilty of killing John F. Kennedy assassin Lee Harvey Oswald.
- March 15 – Richard Burton and Elizabeth Taylor marry (for the first time) in Montreal.
- March 18 – Approximately 50 Moroccan students broke into the embassy of Morocco in the Soviet Union and staged an all-day sit-in protesting against sentencing of 11 people to death for the alleged assassination attempt of King Hassan II of Morocco.
- March 19 – The American Geraldine Jerrie Mock is the first woman to fly solo around the world from March 19 to April 17.
- March 20–June 6 – The first United Nations Conference on Trade and Development takes place.
- March 20 – The precursor of the European Space Agency, ESRO (European Space Research Organization) is established per an agreement signed on June 14, 1962.
- March 21 – *Non ho l'età* by Gigliola Cinquetti (music by Nicola Salerno, text by Mario Panzeri) wins the Eurovision Song Contest 1964 for Italy.

- March 26 – U.S. Defense Secretary Robert McNamara delivers an address that reiterates American determination to give South Vietnam increased military and economic aid, in its war against the Communist insurgency.
- March 27 (Good Friday) – The Great Alaskan earthquake, the second most powerful known (and the most powerful earthquake in the United States) at a magnitude of 9.2, strikes Southcentral Alaska, killing 125 people and inflicting massive damage to the city of Anchorage.
- March 28
  - King Saud of Saudi Arabia abdicates the throne.
  - Radio Caroline becomes the United Kingdom's first "Pirate" radio station, broadcasting from a ship anchored just outside UK territorial waters on the east coast.
- March 30 – Merv Griffin's game show *Jeopardy!* debuts on NBC; Art Fleming is its first host.
- March 31 – The military overthrows Brazilian President João Goulart in a coup, starting 21 years of dictatorship in Brazil. It ends in 1985.

April

- April 1 – Deployed military rule in Brazil ended the then government democratically elected president João Goulart.
- April 2 – Mrs. Malcolm Peabody, 72, mother of Massachusetts Governor Endicott Peabody, is released on $450 bond after spending 2 days in a St. Augustine, Florida

jail, for participating in an anti-segregation demonstration there.

- April 4
  - The Beatles hold the top 5 positions in the Billboard Top 40 singles in America, an unprecedented achievement. The top songs in America as listed on April 4, in order, are: Can't Buy Me Love, Twist and Shout, She Loves You, I Want to Hold Your Hand, and Please Please Me.
  - Three high school friends in Hoboken, N.J., open the first Blimpie on Washington Street.

April 8: Gemini 1 launched.

- April 6 – Jigme Palden Dorji, premier of the Himalayan kingdom of Bhutan, is shot dead by an unidentified assassin in Puncholing, near the Indian border.
- April 7 – IBM announces the System/360.
- April 8
  - Four of 5 railroad operating unions strike against the Illinois Central Railroad without warning, bringing to a head a 5-year dispute over railroad work rules.
  - Gemini 1 is launched, the first unmanned test of the 2-man spacecraft.
  - *From Russia with Love* premiers in U.S. movie theaters.

- April 9 – The United Nations Security Council adopts by a 9–0 vote a resolution deploring a British air attack on a fort in Yemen 12 days earlier, in which 25 persons were reported killed.
- April 10 – Demolition of the Polo Grounds sports stadium commences in New York City.
- April 11 – The Brazilian Congress elects Field Marshal Humberto de Alencar Castelo Branco as President of Brazil.
- April 12 – In Detroit, Malcolm X delivers a speech entitled "The Ballot or the Bullet"
- April 13
    - The 36th Academy Awards ceremony is held.
    - Sidney Poitier is the first African-American to win an Academy Award in the category Best Actor in a Leading Role in *Lilies of the Field*.
- April 14 – A Delta rocket's third-stage motor ignites prematurely in an assembly room at Cape Canaveral, killing 3.
- April 16
    - The Rolling Stones release their debut album, *The Rolling Stones*.
    - Sentences totaling 307 years are passed on 12 men who stole £2.6m in used bank notes, after holding up the night mail train traveling from Glasgow to London in August 1963 – a heist that became known as the Great Train Robbery.
- April 17
    - In the United States, the Ford Mustang is officially unveiled to the public.
    - Shea Stadium opens in Flushing, New York.

- April 19 – In Laos, the coalition government of Prince Souvanna Phouma is deposed by a right-wing military group, led by Brig. Gen. Kouprasith Abhay. Not supported by the U.S., the coup is ultimately unsuccessful, and Souvanna Phouma is reinstated, remaining Prime Minister until 1975.
- April 20
  - U.S. President Lyndon Johnson in New York, and Soviet Premier Nikita Khrushchev in Moscow, simultaneously announce plans to cut back production of materials for making nuclear weapons.
  - Nelson Mandela makes his "I Am Prepared to Die" speech at the opening of the Rivonia Trial, a key event for the anti-apartheid movement.
  - BBC2 starts broadcasting in the UK.
- April 22
  - British businessman Greville Wynne, imprisoned in Moscow since 1963 for spying, is exchanged for Soviet spy Gordon Lonsdale.

April 22: 1964 New York World's Fair

-
  - The 1964 New York World's Fair opens to celebrate the 300th anniversary of New Amsterdam being taken over by British forces under the Duke of York (later King

James II) and being renamed New York in 1664. The fair runs until October 18, 1964 and reopens April 21, 1965, finally closing October 17, 1965. (Not sanctioned, due to being within 10 years of the Seattle World's Fair in 1962, some countries decline, but many countries have pavilions with exotic crafts, art and food.)

- April 25 – Thieves steal the head of the Little Mermaid statue in Copenhagen, Denmark (Henrik Bruun confesses in 1997).
- April 26 – Tanganyika and Zanzibar merge to form Tanzania.

May

- May 1 – At 4:00 a.m., John George Kemeny and Thomas Eugene Kurtz ran the first computer program written in BASIC (Beginners' All-purpose Symbolic Instruction Code), an easy to learn high level programming language which they created. BASIC was eventually included on many computers and even some games consoles.
- May 2
  - Senator Barry Goldwater receives more than 75% of the votes in the Texas Republican Presidential primary.
  - Some 400–1,000 students march through Times Square, New York and another 700 in San Francisco, in the first major student demonstration against the Vietnam War. Smaller marches also occur in Boston, Seattle, and Madison, Wisconsin.
  - Henry Hezekiah Dee and Charles Eddie Moore, hitchhiking in Meadville, Mississippi, are kidnapped

and beaten by members of the Ku Klux Klan. Their badly decomposed bodies are found by chance 2 months later in July, during the search for 3 civil rights workers – Chaney, Goodman, and Schwerner.

- May 4 – The United States Congress recognized Bourbon whiskey as a "distinctive product of the United States".
- May 7
  - Pacific Air Lines Flight 773 crashes near San Ramon, California, killing all 44 aboard; the FBI later reports that a cockpit recorder tape indicates that the pilot and co-pilot had been shot by a suicidal passenger.
  - At a mail rockets demonstration by Gerhard Zucker on Hasselkopf Mountain near Braunlage (Lower Saxonia, Germany), 3 persons are killed by a rocket explosion.
- May 9 – South Korean President Park Chung-hee reshuffles his Cabinet, after a series of student demonstrations against his efforts to restore diplomatic and trade relations with Japan.
- May 11 – Terence Conran opens the first Habitat store on London's Fulham Road.
- May 12 – Twelve young men in New York City publicly burn their draft cards to protest the war; the first such act of war resistance.
- May 19 – The United States State Department says that more than 40 hidden microphones have been found embedded in the walls of the U.S. Embassy in Moscow.
- May 23
  - Mrs. Madeline Dassault, 63, wife of a French plane manufacturer and politician, is kidnapped while leaving her car in front of her Paris home; she is found

unharmed the next day in a farmhouse 27 miles (43 km) from Paris.

- o Pablo Picasso paints his fourth *Head of a Bearded Man*.
- May 24–25 – The crowd at a football match in Lima, Peru riots over a referee's decision in the Peru-Argentina game; 319 are killed, 500 injured.
- May 26 – Nelson Rockefeller defeats Barry Goldwater in the Oregon Republican primary, slowing but not stalling Goldwater's drive toward the nomination.
- May 27 – Prime Minister of India Jawaharlal Nehru dies; he is succeeded by Lal Bahadur Shastri.
- May 28 – The Charter of the Palestine Liberation Organization (PLO) is released by Arab League.
- May 30 – Eddie Sachs and Dave MacDonald are killed in a fiery crash during the 1964 Indianapolis 500.

June

- June 2
  - o Senator Barry Goldwater wins the California Republican Presidential primary, making him the overwhelming favorite for the nomination.
  - o Five million shares of stock in the Communications Satellite Corporation (Comsat) are offered for sale at $20 a share, and the issue is quickly sold out.
- June 3 – South Korean President Park Chung-hee declares martial law in Seoul, after 10,000 student demonstrators overpower police.

- June 6 – With a temporary order, the rocket launches at Cuxhaven are terminated.
- June 9 – In Federal Court in Kansas City, Kansas, army deserter George John Gessner, 28, is convicted of passing United States secrets to the Soviet Union.
- June 10
    - The U.S. Senate votes cloture of the Civil Rights Bill after a 75-day filibuster.
    - The Deacons for Defense and Justice (Black self-defense organization) is founded in Jonesboro, Louisiana.
- June 11
    - Greece rejects direct talks with Turkey over Cyprus.
    - Cologne school massacre: In Cologne, West Germany, Walter Seifert attacks students and teachers in an elementary school with a flamethrower, killing 10 and injuring 21.
- June 12
    - Pennsylvania Governor William Scranton announces his candidacy for the Republican Presidential nomination, as part of a 'stop-Goldwater' movement.
    - Nelson Mandela and 7 others are sentenced to life imprisonment in South Africa, and sent to the Robben Island prison.
- June 16 – Keith Bennett, 12, is abducted by Myra Hindley and Ian Brady. As of 2016, his body has not been recovered.
- June 17 – Author Ken Kesey and his Merry Pranksters embark on their cross-country trip aboard Further (bus) spreading the gospel of LSD.
- June 19 – U.S. Senator Edward Kennedy, 32, is seriously injured in a private plane crash at Southampton, Massachusetts; the pilot is killed.

- June 20 – The Ford GT40 makes its first appearance at the 24 Hours of Le Mans. It does not see its first victory, however, until 1966. At the same event, the AC Cobra wins its class in its second Le Mans appearance.
- June 21
    - Three civil rights workers, Michael Schwerner, Andrew Goodman, and James Chaney, are murdered near Philadelphia, Mississippi, by local Klansmen and a deputy sheriff.
    - Spain beats the Soviet Union 2–1 to win the 1964 European Nations Cup.
    - Jim Bunning pitches a perfect game for the Philadelphia Phillies, the first in the National League since 1880.
- June 26 – Moise Tshombe returns to the Democratic Republic of the Congo from exile in Spain.
- June 29 – Manx Radio commences broadcasting from Douglas, Isle of Man after receiving its first Low power broadcast licence from the United Kingdom's General Post Office.

July

- July 2 – President Lyndon Johnson signs the Civil Rights Act of 1964 into law, officially abolishing racial segregation in the United States.
- July 6 – Malawi receives its independence from the United Kingdom.

- July 8 – U.S. military personnel announce that U.S. casualties in Vietnam have risen to 1,387, including 399 dead and 17 MIA.
- July 16 – At the Republican National Convention in San Francisco, U.S. presidential nominee Barry Goldwater declares that "extremism in the defense of liberty is no vice", and "moderation in the pursuit of justice is no virtue".
- July 18
    - Six days of race riots begin in Harlem.
    - Judith Graham Pool publishes her discovery of cryoprecipitate, a frozen blood clotting product made from plasma primarily to treat hemophiliacs around the world.
    - "False Hare" is the final Warner Bros. cartoon with "target" titles.
- July 19 – Vietnam War: At a rally in Saigon, South Vietnamese Prime Minister Nguyễn Khánh calls for expanding the war into North Vietnam.
- July 20
    - Vietnam War: Viet Cong forces attack a provincial capital, killing 11 South Vietnamese military personnel and 40 civilians (30 of which are children).
    - The National Movement of the Revolution is instituted as the sole legal political party in the Republic of the Congo.
- July 21 – Race riots begin in Singapore between ethnic Chinese and Malays.
- July 22 – The second meeting of the Organisation of African Unity is held.
- July 24 – There is a minor criticality accident at a United Nuclear Corporation Fuels recovery plant in Wood River

Junction, Richmond, Rhode Island. 37-year-old Robert Peabody dies two days after the incident.

- July 27 – Vietnam War: The U.S. sends 5,000 more military advisers to South Vietnam, bringing the total number of United States forces in Vietnam to 21,000.
- July 31 – Ranger program: Ranger 7 sends back the first close-up photographs of the Moon (images are 1,000 times clearer than anything ever seen from Earth-bound telescopes).

August

- August 1
  - The Final Looney Tune, "Señorella and the Glass Huarache", is released before the Warner Bros. Cartoon Division is shut down by Jack Warner.
- August 4
  - American civil rights movement: The bodies of murdered civil rights workers Michael Schwerner, Andrew Goodman and James Chaney are found.
  - Vietnam War: United States destroyers USS *Maddox* and USS *Turner Joy* are attacked in the Gulf of Tonkin. Air support from the carrier USS *Ticonderoga* sinks one gunboat, while the other two leave the battle.
- August 5
  - Vietnam War: Operation Pierce Arrow – Aircraft from carriers USS *Ticonderoga* and USS *Constellation* bomb North Vietnam in retaliation for strikes against U.S. destroyers in the Gulf of Tonkin.

- The Simba rebel army in the Democratic Republic of the Congo captures Stanleyville, and takes 1,000 Western hostages.
- August 7 – Vietnam War: The United States Congress passes the Gulf of Tonkin Resolution, giving U.S. President Lyndon B. Johnson broad war powers to deal with North Vietnamese attacks on U.S. forces.
- August 8 – A Rolling Stones gig in Scheveningen gets out of control. Riot police end the gig after about 15 minutes, upon which spectators start to fight the riot police.
- August 13 – Murderers Gwynne Owen Evans and Peter Anthony Allen become the last people to be executed in the United Kingdom.
- August 16 – Vietnam War: In a coup, General Nguyễn Khánh replaces Dương Văn Minh as South Vietnam's chief of state and establishes a new constitution, drafted partly by the U.S. Embassy.
- August 17 – Margaret Harshaw, Metropolitan Opera soprano, sings the role of Turandot in Puccini's opera *Turandot* at the New York World's Fair.
- August 18 – The International Olympic Committee bans South Africa from the Tokyo Olympics on the grounds that its teams are racially segregated.
- August 20 – The International Telecommunications Satellite Consortium (Intelsat) began to work.
- August 22
  - Fannie Lou Hamer, civil rights activist and Vice Chair of the Mississippi Freedom Democratic Party, addresses the Credentials Committee of the Democratic National Convention, challenging the all-white Mississippi delegation.

- Goalkeeper Derek Foster of Sunderland becomes the youngest-ever player to play in the Football League, aged 15 years and 185 days.
- August 24–27 – The Democratic National Convention in Atlantic City nominates incumbent President Lyndon B. Johnson for a full term, and U.S. Senator Hubert Humphrey of Minnesota as his running mate.
- August 27 – Walt Disney's *Mary Poppins* has its world premiere in Los Angeles. It will go on to become Disney's biggest moneymaker, and winner of 5 Academy Awards, including a Best Actress award for Julie Andrews, who accepted the part after she was passed over by Jack L. Warner for the leading role of Eliza Doolittle in the film version of *My Fair Lady*. *Mary Poppins* is the first Disney film to be nominated for Best Picture.
- August 28–30 – Philadelphia 1964 race riot: Tensions between African American residents and police lead to 341 injuries and 774 arrests.

September

- September 2 – Indian Hungry generation poets are arrested on charges of conspiracy against the state and obscenity in literature.
- September 4 – The Forth Road Bridge opens over the Firth of Forth.
- September 10 – The African Development Bank (AfDB) is founded.

- September 11 – In Jacksonville, Florida, John Lennon announces that the Beatles will not play to a segregated audience.
- September 14
    - The third period of the Second Vatican Council opens.
    - The London *Daily Herald* ceases publication, replaced by *The Sun*.
- September 16 – *Shindig!* premieres on the *ABC*, featuring the top musical acts of the Sixties.
- September 17
    - *Goldfinger* opens in the UK.
    - *Bewitched*, starring Elizabeth Montgomery, premieres on ABC.
- September 18 – In Athens, King Constantine II of Greece marries Princess Anne-Marie of Denmark, who becomes Europe's youngest Queen at age 18 years, 19 days.
    - *Jonny Quest* premieres on ABC; featured voices include Mike Road, Tim Matheson, Don Messick, John Stephenson, and Danny Bravo.
- September 20 – At the autumnal equinox, the Order of Bards, Ovates and Druids (OBOD) is founded in England.
- September 21
    - The island of Malta obtains independence from the United Kingdom.
    - The North American XB-70 Valkyrie makes its first flight at Palmdale, California.
- September 24 – The Warren Commission Report, the first official investigation of the assassination of United States President John F. Kennedy, is published.
- September 25 – The Mozambican War of Independence is launched by FRELIMO.

- September – Pete Townshend of The Who destroys his first guitar in the name of auto-destructive art at the Railway Hotel, London.

October

1964 Summer Olympics

- October – Dr. Robert Moog demonstrates the prototype Moog synthesizer.
- October 1
  - Three thousand student activists at University of California, Berkeley, surround and block a police car from taking a CORE volunteer arrested for not showing his ID, when he violated a ban on outdoor activist card tables. This protest eventually explodes into the Berkeley Free Speech Movement.
  - The *Shinkansen* high-speed rail system, the world's first such system, is inaugurated in Japan, for the first sector between Tokyo and Osaka.

- October 2 – The Kinks release their first album, *Kinks*.
- October 5
    - Twenty-three men and thirty-one women escape to West Berlin through a narrow tunnel under the Berlin Wall.
    - Elizabeth II and The Duke of Edinburgh begin an 8-day visit to Canada.
- October 10–24 – The 1964 Summer Olympics are held in Tokyo.
- October 12 – The Soviet Union launches *Voskhod 1* into Earth orbit as the first spacecraft with a multi-person crew and the first flight without space suits. The flight is cut short and lands again on October 13 after 16 orbits.
- October 14 – American civil rights movement leader Dr. Martin Luther King Jr. becomes the youngest recipient of the Nobel Peace Prize, which was awarded to him for leading non-violent resistance to end racial prejudice in the United States.
- October 14–15 – Nikita Khrushchev is deposed as leader of the Soviet Union; Leonid Brezhnev and Alexei Kosygin assume power.
- October 15
    - The Labour Party wins the parliamentary elections in the United Kingdom, ending 13 years of Conservative Party rule. The new prime minister is Harold Wilson.
    - Craig Breedlove's jet-powered car *Spirit of America* goes out of control in Bonneville Salt Flats in Utah and makes skid marks 9.6 km long.
- October 16
    - Harold Wilson becomes British Prime Minister after leading the Labour Party to a narrow election win over

the Tory government of Sir Alec Douglas-Home, which had been in power for 13 years and had four different leaders during that time.

- 596: The People's Republic of China explodes an atomic bomb in Sinkiang.

- October 18 – The New York World's Fair closes for the year (it reopens April 21, 1965).
- October 21 – The film version of the hit Broadway stage musical *My Fair Lady* premieres in New York City. The movie stars Audrey Hepburn in the role of Eliza Doolittle and Rex Harrison repeating his stage performance as Professor Henry Higgins, and which will win him his only Academy Award for Best Actor. The film will win seven other Academy Awards, including Best Picture, but Audrey Hepburn will not be nominated. Critics interpret this as a rebuke to Jack L. Warner for choosing Ms. Hepburn over Julie Andrews.
- October 22
    - Canada: A Federal Multi-Party Parliamentary Committee selects a design to become the new official Flag of Canada.
    - A 5.3 kiloton nuclear device is detonated at the Tatum Salt Dome, 21 miles (34 km) from Hattiesburg, Mississippi as part of the Vela Uniform program. This test is the Salmon phase of the Atomic Energy Commission's Project Dribble.
- October 24 – Northern Rhodesia, a former British protectorate, becomes the independent Republic of Zambia, ending 73 years of British rule.

- October 26 – Eric Edgar Cooke becomes the last man executed in Western Australia, for murdering 8 citizens in Perth between 1959 and 1963.
- October 27 – In the Democratic Republic of the Congo, rebel leader Christopher Gbenye takes 60 Americans and 800 Belgians hostage.
- October 29 – A collection of irreplaceable gemstones, including the 565 carats (113.0 g) Star of India, is stolen from the American Museum of Natural History in New York City.
- October 31 – Campaigning at Madison Square Garden, New York, U.S. President Lyndon Johnson pledges the creation of the Great Society.

November

- November 1 – Mortar fire from North Vietnamese forces rains on the Bien Hoa Air Base, killing four U.S. servicemen, wounding 72, and destroying five B-57 jet bombers and other planes.
- November 3
  - United States presidential election, 1964: Incumbent President Lyndon B. Johnson defeats Republican challenger Barry Goldwater with over 60 percent of the popular vote.
  - The Bolivian government of President Víctor Paz Estenssoro is overthrown by a military rebellion led by General Alfredo Ovando Candía, commander-in-chief of the armed forces.

- November 5 – Mariner program: Mariner 3, a U.S. space probe intended for Mars, is launched from Cape Kennedy but fails.
- November 9 – The House of Commons of the United Kingdom votes to abolish the death penalty for murder in Britain.
- November 10 – Australia partially reintroduces compulsory military service due to the Indonesian Confrontation.
- November 13 – Bob Pettit (St. Louis Hawks) becomes the first American National Basketball Association player to score 20,000 points.
- November 19 – The United States Department of Defense announces the closing of 95 military bases and facilities, including the Brooklyn Navy Yard, the Brooklyn Army Terminal, and Fort Jay, New York.
- November 21
  - Second Vatican Council: The third period of the Catholic Church's ecumenical council closes. *Lumen gentium*, the Dogmatic Constitution on the Church, is promulgated.
  - The Verrazano–Narrows Bridge across New York Bay opens to traffic (the world's longest suspension bridge at this time).
- November 24 – Belgian paratroopers and mercenaries capture Stanleyville, but a number of hostages die in the fighting, among them American Evangelical Covenant Church missionary Dr. Paul Carlson.
- November 28
  - Mariner program: NASA launches the Mariner 4 space probe from Cape Kennedy toward Mars to take television pictures of that planet in July 1965.

- Vietnam War: United States National Security Council members, including Robert McNamara, Dean Rusk, and Maxwell Taylor, agree to recommend a plan for a 2-stage escalation of bombing in North Vietnam, to President Lyndon B. Johnson.
- France performs an underground nuclear test at Ecker, Algeria.

December

- December 1
  - Gustavo Díaz Ordaz takes office as President of Mexico.
  - Vietnam War: U.S. President Lyndon B. Johnson and his top-ranking advisers meet to discuss plans to bomb North Vietnam (after some debate, they agree on a 2-phase bombing plan).
- December 3
  - Berkeley Free Speech Movement: Police arrest about 800 students at the University of California, Berkeley, following their takeover of and massive sit-in at the Sproul Hall administration building. The sit-in most directly protested the U.C. Regents' decision to punish student activists for what many thought had been justified civil disobedience earlier in the conflict.
  - The Danish football club Brøndby IF was founded as a merger between the two local clubs Brøndbyøster Idrætsforening and Brøndbyvester Idrætsforening. The club has won the national championship Danish

Superliga 10 times, and has won the national Danish Cups six times since the club joined the Danish top-flight football league in 1981.

- December 6 – The 1-hour stop-motion animated special *Rudolph the Red-Nosed Reindeer*, based on the popular Christmas song, premieres on NBC. It becomes a beloved Christmas tradition, still being shown on television more than 50 years later.
- December 9 – A Love Supreme recorded by John Coltrane with his quartet at Van Gelder Studio, Englewood Cliffs, New Jersey, United States
- December 10 – Dr. Martin Luther King Jr. is awarded the Nobel Peace Prize in Oslo, Norway.
- December 11
    - Sam Cooke, African-American singer and songwriter was shot and killed at a motel in Los Angeles, California (b. 1931)
- December 11 – Che Guevara addresses the U.N. General Assembly.
- December 12 – Jamhuri Day: Kenya becomes a republic, with Jomo Kenyatta as its first President.
- December 14 – *Heart of Atlanta Motel v. United States* (379 US 241 1964): The U.S. Supreme Court rules that, in accordance with the Civil Rights Act of 1964, establishments providing public accommodation must refrain from racial discrimination.
- December 15 – *The Washington Post* publishes an article about James Hampton, who has built a glittering religious throne out of recycled materials.
- December 18

- In the wake of deadly riots in January over control of the Panama Canal, the U.S. offers to negotiate a new canal treaty.
- The deadly Christmas flood of 1964 begins; It becomes one of the most destructive weather events to affect Oregon in the 20th century.
- December 21
  - The James Bond film *Goldfinger* begins its run in U.S. theaters. It becomes one of the most successful and popular Bond films ever made.
  - The General Dynamics F-111 Aardvark makes its first flight.
- December 22
  - Comedian Lenny Bruce is sentenced to 4 months in prison, concluding a 6-month obscenity trial.
  - A cyclone in the Palk Strait destroys the Indian town of Dhanushkodi, killing 1800 people.
  - The Lockheed SR-71 Blackbird makes its first flight at Palmdale, California.
- December 23 – Wonderful Radio London becomes the United Kingdom's fourth "Pirate" radio station, broadcasting from MV *Galaxy* (a former US Navy minesweeper) anchored off the east coast of England, with an American-style Top 40 ("Fab 40") playlist of popular records.
- December 24 – Bombing of the Brinks Hotel in Saigon.
- December 26 – Lesley Ann Downey, 10, is abducted by Ian Brady and Myra Hindley in Manchester, England.
- December 27 – The Cleveland Browns defeat the Baltimore Colts, 27-0, in the National Football League Championship Game.

- December 30 – United Nations Conference on Trade and Development (UNCTAD) established as a permanent organ of the UN General Assembly.

Date unknown

- Spring – First recognition of cosmic microwave background radiation as a detectable phenomenon.
- Jerome Horwitz synthesizes zidovudine (AZT), an antiviral drug which will later be used in treating HIV.
- Farrington Daniels' book *Direct Use of the Sun's Energy* is published by Yale University Press.
- Rudi Gernreich designs the original monokini topless swimsuit in the U.S.
- The Vishva Hindu Pariṣad is founded in India.
- The Centre for Contemporary Cultural Studies is established at the University of Birmingham, England, by Richard Hoggart.
- Roald Dahl writes *Charlie and the Chocolate Factory*.
- The first fatality occurs at Disneyland. A 15-year-old boy was injured while riding the Matterhorn Bobsleds and died three days later as a result of his injuries.
- The Pontiac GTO, the first vehicle to be officially dubbed a "muscle car", debuts as a trim of the Pontiac Tempest.

Births

January

Nicolas Cage

Penelope Ann Miller

Michelle Obama

- January 1 – Juliana Donald, American actress.
- January 2 – Pernell Whitaker, American boxer
- January 3 – Jon Gibson, American Christian musician

- January 4 – Dot Jones, American actress and retired athlete
- January 5 – Miguel Ángel Jiménez, Spanish golfer
- January 6
  - Colin Cowherd, American talk show host
  - Henry Maske, German boxer
  - Jacqueline DeLois Moore, American wrestler
  - Rafael Vidal, Venezuelan swimmer and sports commentator (d. 2005)
- January 7 – Nicolas Cage, American actor
- January 12 – Jeff Bezos, American Internet entrepreneur
- January 13
  - Penelope Ann Miller, American actress
  - Bill Bailey, British comedian
- January 15 – Osmo Tapio Räihälä, Finnish composer
- January 16 – Chris Dittmar, Australian squash player
- January 17
  - Michelle Fairley, Northern Irish actress
  - Michelle Obama, First Lady of the United States
- January 18 – Jane Horrocks, British actress
- January 19 – Ricardo Arjona, Guatemalan singer
- January 23
  - Mariska Hargitay, American actress
  - Kelly Parsons, American actress and model
- January 27 – Bridget Fonda, American actress
- January 29 – Andre Reed, NFL player, 2014 Pro Football Hall of Fame inductee
- January 31 – Jeff Hanneman, American rock guitarist (Slayer) (d. 2013)

February

Matt Dillon

- February 5
  - Laura Linney, American actress
  - Duff McKagan, American rock musician, songwriter
- February 8 – German Gref, Minister of Economics and Trade of Russia
- February 10
  - Glenn Beck, American conservative broadcaster
  - John Campbell, New Zealand broadcaster
- February 11
  - Sarah Palin, American politician, former Governor of Alaska
  - Ken Shamrock, American mixed martial arts fighter
- February 15
  - Chris Farley, American actor and comedian (d. 1997)
  - Mark Price, American basketball player
- February 16
  - Bebeto, Brazilian footballer
  - Christopher Eccleston, British actor
- February 18
  - Matt Dillon, American actor

- ○ Tommy Scott, British musician and frontman of Space
- February 19
  - ○ Jonathan Lethem, American author
  - ○ Richard A. Scott, American illustrator
- February 20 – Willie Garson, American character actor
- February 22 – Diane Charlemagne, English singer (52nd Street, Urban Cookie Collective) (d. 2015)
- February 24
  - ○ Todd Field, American actor and director
  - ○ Ute Geweniger, German swimmer
- February 25 – Lee Evans, British comedian and actor
- February 28 – Djamolidine Abdoujaparov, Uzbekistan cyclist

March

Juliette Binoche

Steve Wilkos

Rob Lowe

Prince Edward, Earl of Wessex

- March 4
  - Paul Bostaph, American drummer
  - Tom Lampkin, American baseball player
- March 6 – Skip Ewing, American country singer
- March 7
  - Bret Easton Ellis, American author
  - Vladimir Smirnov, Kazakh cross-country skier
  - Wanda Sykes, African-American comedian and actress
- March 9
  - Juliette Binoche, French actress
  - Steve Wilkos, American retired police officer; talk show host
- March 10
  - Neneh Cherry, Swedish-born singer-songwriter

- Prince Edward, Earl of Wessex, British prince and third son (youngest child) of Elizabeth II and The Duke of Edinburgh
- March 11 – Shane Richie, British actor
- March 16
  - Pascal Richard, Swiss road bicycle racer
  - Gore Verbinski, American film director
- March 17 – Rob Lowe, American actor
- March 18
  - Bonnie Blair, American speed skater
  - Mika Kanai, Japanese voice actress
  - Rozalla, Zambian singer
- March 19
  - Yoko Kanno, Japanese composer
  - Jake Weber, English actor
- March 20 – Michael Keith Smith, American bass player and builder
- March 23 – Hope Davis, American actress
- March 24 – Liz McColgan, British long-distance runner athlete
- March 25
  - Lisa Gay Hamilton, American actress
  - Vince Offer, American writer, director, comedian and pitchman
- March 26
  - Martin Donnelly, Northern Irish racecar driver
  - Ed Wasser, American actor
- March 29
  - Ming Tsai, Chinese-American chef
  - Michael A. Jackson, former sheriff of Prince George's County, Maryland

- March 30
  - Tracy Chapman, African-American singer
  - Sigurd Haveland, Gibraltarian triathlete and cyclist
- March 31
  - David Wyman (American football), Former American football player

April

David Cross

David Woodard

Russell Crowe

Hank Azaria

- April 1 – Erik Breukink, Dutch cyclist and manager
- April 3
  - Nigel Farage, English politician and MEP, head of UK Independence Party (UKIP)
  - Gary Love, British actor and film director
  - Bjarne Riis, Danish cyclist
- April 4 – David Cross, American actor and comedian
- April 6 – David Woodard, American businessman
- April 7
  - Russell Crowe, New Zealand-born actor
  - Steve Graves, Canadian ice hockey player
- April 8 – Lisa Guerrero, Hispanic American actress, model and sportscaster/reporter
- April 13 – Caroline Rhea, Canadian actress and comedian
- April 14 – Takumi Yamazaki, Japanese voice actress
- April 16 – Esbjörn Svensson Swedish jazz pianist (d. 2008)
- April 18 – Lourenço Mutarelli, Brazilian underground comic book writer
- April 19 – Harris Barton, American football player
- April 20
  - Crispin Glover, American actor
  - Andy Serkis, English actor

- April 21 – Ludmila Engquist, Russian-born Swedish athlete
- April 24 – Augusta Read Thomas, American composer
- April 25
    - Hank Azaria, American actor, voice artist and comedian
    - Andy Bell, English singer and songwriter
- April 28 – L'Wren Scott, American fashion designer (d. 2014)
- April 29
    - Federico Castelluccio, Italian-born actor
    - Radek Jaroš, Czech mountaineer
- April 30 – Misa Watanabe, Japanese voice actress

May

Stephen Colbert

Lenny Kravitz

- May 1 – Yvonne van Gennip, Dutch speed-skater
- May 3 – Ron Hextall, Canadian ice hockey player

- May 4 – Zsuzsa Mathe, Hungarian born painter and visual artist, founder of Transrealism
- May 5
  - Heike Henkel, German high jumper
  - Minami Takayama, Japanese voice actress and singer (Two-Mix and DoCo)
- May 6 – Dana Hill, American voice actress (d. 1996)
- May 7
  - Doug Benson, American comedian
  - Ronnie Harmon, American football player
  - Leslie O'Neal, American football player
- May 8
  - Melissa Gilbert, American actress and president of the Screen Actors Guild
  - Bobby Labonte, American race car driver
  - Dave Rowntree, English drummer (Blur)
- May 10 – Mark Andre, French-born German composer
- May 11 – John Parrott, English snooker player
- May 13 – Stephen Colbert, American comedian and television personality; host of The Late Show with Stephen Colbert
- May 14 – Suzy Kolber, American sportscaster
- May 16 – John Salley, American basketball player and talk show host
- May 20 – Charles Edward Maurice Spencer, 9th Earl Spencer, British aristocrat, author, print journalist and broadcaster. Younger brother of Diana, Princess of Wales.
- May 21 – Danny Bailey, English footballer
- May 22 – Marcus Dupree, American football player
- May 23 – Ruth Metzler-Arnold, member of the Swiss Federal Council

- May 24 – Adrian Moorhouse, British swimmer
- May 26
  - Caitlín R. Kiernan, American author and paleontologist
  - Lenny Kravitz, American guitarist and singer
- May 27 – Adam Carolla, American comedic radio personality and television personality
- May 28 – Jeff Fenech, Australian boxer
- May 30 – Wynonna Judd, American country singer

June

Courteney Cox

Boris Johnson

- June 1 – Deirdre Bolton, American broadcast journalist and business news and commentator
- June 3 – James Purefoy, British actor
-

- June 5
  - Dukagjin Pupovci, Kosovo Albanian professor
  - Rick Riordan, American author
- June 6 – Guru Josh, British musician (d. 2015)
- June 7
  - Gia Carides, Greek-Australian actress
  - Petr Hruška, Czech poet
- June 9 – Gloria Reuben, Canadian-American actress
- June 13 – Kathy Burke, English actress and comedian
- June 13 – Lance Mountain, American skateboarder
- June 15
  - Courteney Cox, American actress
  - Michael Laudrup, Danish footballer and manager
- June 16 – Martin Streek, Canadian radio personality (d. 2009)
- June 17 – Erin Murphy, American actress
- June 19
  - Boris Johnson, American-born British politician, former Mayor of London (2008-2016)
  - Laura Ingraham, American radio host and political commentator
- June 21 – Doug Savant, American actor
- June 22
  - Amy Brenneman, American actress
  - Dan Brown, American author
- June 23
  - Clete Blakeman, American football official
  - Lou Yun, Chinese gymnast
- June 25 – Johnny Herbert, English race car driver
- June 26 – Tommi Mäkinen, Finnish rally driver
- June 27 – Kai Diekmann, German journalist
- June 28 – Mark Grace, American baseball player

July

Courtney Love

John Leguizamo

David Spade

Sandra Bullock

Mary-Louise Parker

- July 1 – Paul Coyne, American TV producer and editor
- July 1 – Bernard Laporte, French rugby player and coach
- July 2 – José and Ozzie Canseco, Cuban-born American baseball players; twin brothers
- July 3
  - Joanne Harris, English novelist
  - Yeardley Smith, American voice actress
- July 4 – Martin Flood, Australian quiz show winner
- July 5 – Jimmy Demers, American singer/songwriter
- July 7 – Karina Galvez, Ecuadorian poet
- July 9 – Courtney Love, American musician/actress
- July 11 – Craig Charles, British actor
- July 12 – Gaby Roslin, British TV presenter
-

- July 16
  - Andy Abraham, British singer
  - Miguel Indurain, Spanish cyclist
- July 17
  - Heather Langenkamp, American actress
  - Craig Morgan, American country music singer-songwriter
- July 18 – Wendy Williams, African-American former radio host and current talk show host
- July 19 – Masahiko Kondō, Japanese singer
- July 20 – Chris Cornell, American singer
- July 21 – Ross Kemp, British actor
- July 22
  - Adam Godley, British actor
  - Bonnie Langford, British actress
  - John Leguizamo, Colombian-American actor
  - David Spade, American comedian, actor and television personality
- July 23 – Nick Menza, German-born American drummer (Megadeth) (d. 2016)
- July 24 – Barry Bonds, African-American baseball player
- July 25 – Lisa LaFlamme, Canadian journalist and news anchor
- July 26
  - Sandra Bullock, American actress
  - Anne Provoost, Belgian author
- July 30
  - Vivica A. Fox, American actress
  - Jürgen Klinsmann, German footballer-manager and retired player
- July 31 – C.C. Catch, Dutch-born German singer

August

- August 2 – Mary-Louise Parker, American actress
- August 3
  - Lucky Dube, South African reggae musician (d. 2007)
  - Ye Qiaobo, Chinese speed skater
  - Abhisit Vejjajiva, Thai former Prime Minister
- August 5 – Adam Yauch, American rapper (Beastie Boys) (d. 2012)
- August 6
  - Gary Conrad, American animator
  - Gary Valenciano, Filipino musician
- August 8
  - Nina Hoekman, Dutch draughts players (d. 2014)
  - Jan Josef Liefers, German actor, producer, director and musician
- August 9
  - Brett Hull, Canadian hockey player
  - William Martens, American computer engineer
- August 10 – Hiro Takahashi, Japanese singer (d. 2005)
- August 15 – Melinda Gates, American wife of Bill Gates
- August 16 – Jimmy Arias, American tennis player
- August 19 – Dermott Brereton, Australian rules footballer
- August 22
  - Diane Setterfield, British author
  - Mats Wilander, Swedish tennis player
- August 24 – Salizhan Sharipov, Russian cosmonaut
- August 25 – Maxim Kontsevich, Russian mathematician
- August 26
  - Dave Boyes, Canadian male rower
  - Kevin Burns, American politician

- Allegra Huston, English-American author
- Bobby Jurasin, Canadian football defensive lineman
- Chad Kreuter, Major League Baseball catcher
- Zadok Malka, Israeli footballer
- Torsten Schmitz, German boxer
- Carsten Wolf, German male cyclist
- August 27 – Paul Bernardo, Canadian serial killer and rapist

September

Keanu Reeves

Roberto Fico

Maggie Cheung

Monica Bellucci

- September 1
  - Brian Bellows, Canadian ice hockey player
  - Ray D'Arcy, Irish radio and television host
  - Holly Golightly, American author and illustrator
  - Nabeel Rajab, Bahraini activist
  - Charlie Robison, American singer-songwriter and guitarist
- September 2
  - Andrea Illy, Italian businessman
  - Keanu Reeves, Canadian actor-musician
- September 3
  - Adam Curry, American-Dutch businessman and television host, co-founded mevio
  - Spike Feresten, American screenwriter and producer

- Junaid Jamshed, Pakistani singer-songwriter and guitarist (Vital Signs)
- Holt McCallany, American actor
- Nigel Rhodes, English actor and guitarist
- September 4- Anthony Weiner, U.S. Representative for New York's 9th congressional district
- September 6 – Todd Palin, American husband of former governor Sarah Palin
- September 7 – Andy Hug, Swiss Seidokaikan karateka and kickboxer (d. 2000)
- September 8
  - Michael Johns, American health care executive and Presidential speechwriter
  - Raven, American professional wrestler
- September 11 – Ellis Burks, American baseball player
- September 14 – Faith Ford, American actress
- September 15 – Robert Fico, Prime Minister of Slovakia
- September 19 – Trisha Yearwood, American country singer
- September 20 – Maggie Cheung, Hong Kong actress
- September 22
  - Ian Culverhouse, English footballer
  - Juha Turunen, Finnish politician turned criminal
- September 23 – Koshi Inaba, Japanese singer (B'z)
- September 24 – Rafael Palmeiro, Cuban-American baseball player
- September 25 – Kikuko Inoue, Japanese singer and voice actress
- September 27 – Stephan Jenkins, American musician
- September 28 – Janeane Garofalo, American actress and comedian
-

- September 30
  - Trey Anastasio, American musician
  - Monica Bellucci, Italian actress and model

October

Nicole

David Kaye

Grant Gee

- October 1 – Harry Hill, English comedian, writer and actor
- October 2
  - Dirk Brinkmann, German field hockey player
  - Makharbek Khadartsev, Russian free-style wrestler
- October 3 – Clive Owen, English actor
- October 4
  - Francis Magalona, Filipino rapper (d. 2009)

- Yvonne Murray, Scottish athlete
- October 5 – Keiji Fujiwara, Japanese voice actor
- October 8
  - Martin Marquez, English actor
  - CeCe Winans, African-American Christian musician
- October 10
  - Quinton Flynn, American voice actor
  - Maxi Gnauck, East German gymnast
- October 13 – Masaya Onosaka, Japanese voice actor
- October 14
  - Joe Girardi, American baseball player-manager
  - David Kaye, Canadian voice actor
  - Jim Rome, American sports T.V. and radio host
- October 18 – John Swasey, American voice actor
- October 19
  - Jorge Luis González, Cuban boxer
  - Ty Pennington, American carpenter, model and television personality
- October 22
  - Dražen Petrović, Croatian basketball player (d. 1993)
  - TobyMac, American-born Christian musician
- October 23 – David Sobolov, Canadian voice actor and director
- October 24
  - Rosana Arbelo, Spanish singer and composer
  - Paul Bonwick, Canadian House of Commons member
  - Grant Gee, English film maker, photographer and cinematographer
- October 25 – Nicole, German singer, Eurovision Song Contest 1982 winner

- October 26 – Marc Lépine, Canadian mass murderer (d. 1989)
- October 28 – Onofrio Catacchio, Italian artist
- October 29 – Yasmin Le Bon, British model
- October 31 – Marco van Basten, Dutch footballer and manager

November

Calista Flockhart

Patrick Warburton

Nicholas Patrick

Don Cheadle

- November 1 – Daran Norris, American voice actor
- November 3 – Paprika Steen, Danish actress
- November 4
    - Kurt Krakowian, American child actor
    - Douglas Wilson, American television personality and interior designer
- November 6 – Greg Graffin, American rock musician (Bad Religion)
- November 7 – Dana Plato, American actress (d. 1999)
- November 10
    - Kenny Rogers, American baseball player
    - Magnús Scheving, Icelandic producer
- November 11
    - Calista Flockhart, American actress
    - Ai-Ai delas Alas, Filipino actress
- November 12 – David Ellefson, American rock bassist (Megadeth)
- November 14
    - Rev Run, African-American rapper (Run–D.M.C.)
    - Patrick Warburton, American actor
- November 16 – Diana Krall, Canadian jazz pianist and singer
- November 17 – Mitch Williams, American baseball player

- November 18
  - Rita Cosby, American television personality
  - Seth Joyner, African-American football player
- November 19
  - Susie Dent, British lexicographer
  - Fred Diamond, 21st mathematician-century American
  - Mike Gregory, English rugby player and coach (d. 2007)
  - Shawn Holman, American baseball player
  - Phil Hughes, Irish footballer and coach
  - Eric Musselman, Sacramento Kings head coach
  - Nicholas Patrick, English astronaut
  - Peter Rohde, Carlton Football Club player
- November 21 – Shane Douglas, American wrestler
- November 23 – Boyd Kestner, American actor
- November 24
  - Garret Dillahunt, American actor
  - Alistair McGowan, British actor and comedian
- November 26 – Vreni Schneider, Swiss alpine skier
- November 27 – Robin Givens, African-American actress
- November 28
  - Giorgi Bagaturov, Georgian-Armenian chess grandmaster
  - Michael Bennet, American lawyer, businessman and politician
  - Jorge Capitanich, Argentine politician
  - Ken Charlery, St Lucian international footballer
  - Naoto Hori, Japanese football player
  - Paul Kostacopoulos, American college baseball coach
  - Eugene Licorish, Grenadian long jumper
  - Michelle McKormick, American talk radio personality

- o Oscar Muñoz, Colombian wrestler
- o Zurab Sturua, Georgian chess grandmaster
- o Roy Tarpley, American former professional basketball player
- o Craig Wilson, American professional baseball player
- November 29
  - o Don Cheadle, African-American actor
  - o Cork Graham, American author

December

Sertab Erener

Marisa Tomei

Hape Kerkeling

Stone Cold Steve Austin

- December 1 – Salvatore Schillaci, Italian footballer
- December 3
  - Darryl Hamilton, American baseball player (d. 2015)
  - Scott George Huckabay, American guitarist
- December 4
  - Sertab Erener, Turkish singer-songwriter, Eurovision Song Contest 2003 winner
  - Marisa Tomei, American actress
  - Jonathan Goldstein, American actor
- December 7
  - Roberta Close, Brazilian transgender model
  - Curtis Hughes, American wrestler
  - Peter Laviolette, American ice hockey coach
- December 8 – Teri Hatcher, American actress
- December 9
  - Larry Emdur, Australian game-show host
  - Hape Kerkeling, German actor, presenter and comedian
  - Johannes B. Kerner, German TV personality and sportscaster
  - Paul Landers, German rock musician (Rammstein)
  -

- December 10
  - Bobby Flay, American chef and host
  - Edith González, Mexican actress
- December 11 – John Mark Karr, American murder suspect
- December 12 – Sabu, American professional wrestler
- December 13
  - Hideto "hide" Matsumoto, Japanese musician (d. 1998)
  - Tony Roper, American racing driver (d. 2000)
- December 14
  - Rebecca Gibney, New Zealand-born actress
  - Antje Vowinckel, German radio artist and musician
- December 15
  - Jerry Ball, American football player
  - Denis Scheck, German literary critic and journalist
- December 16
  - Heike Drechsler, German track-and-field athlete
  - Billy Ripken, American baseball player
- December 17 – Frank Musil, Czech ice hockey player and scout
- December 18 – Steve Austin, American professional wrestler
- December 19
  - Ben Becker, German film and theatre actor
  - Arvydas Sabonis, Lithuanian basketball player
- December 22 – Mike Jackson, former MLB pitcher
- December 23 – Eddie Vedder, American rock singer (Pearl Jam)
- December 26 – Elizabeth Kostova, American author
- December 29 – Michael Cudlitz, American actor
- December 30
  - George Newbern, American actor
  - Sophie Ward, British actress

- December 31 – Michael McDonald, American actor and comedian

Date unknown

- Juan Carlos Alom, Cuban photographer
- Fiona Joy Hawkins, Australian composer and pianist
- Jiang Yu, Chinese politician

Deaths

January

Alan Ladd

- January 1 – Bechara El Khoury, President of Lebanon (b. 1890)
- January 8 – Julius Raab, former Chancellor of Austria (b. 1891)
- January 15
  - Tawfiq Canaan, Palestinian doctor (b. 1882)
  - Jack Teagarden, American jazz trombonist (b. 1905)
- January 17 – T. H. White, British author (b. 1906)
- January 19 – Joe Weatherly, NASCAR championship driver (b. 1922)
- January 21 – Joseph Schildkraut, Austrian actor (b. 1896)
- January 22 – Marc Blitzstein, American composer (b. 1905)

- January 27
  - Norman Z. McLeod, American film director (b. 1898)
  - Waite Phillips, American oil man, banker and real estate investor (b. 1883)
- January 29 – Alan Ladd, American actor (b. 1913)

February

- February 5 – Matilde Moisant, American pilot (b. 1878)

Emilio Aguinaldo

- February 6 – Emilio Aguinaldo, First President of the Philippines (b. 1869)
- February 8
  - Boshirō Hosogaya, Japanese admiral (b. 1888)
  - Ernst Kretschmer, German psychiatrist (b. 1888)
- February 10 – Eugen Sänger, Austrian aerospace engineer (b. 1905)
- February 12 – Gerald Gardner (Wiccan), founder of Wiccan religion (b. 1884)
- February 13 – Paulino Alcántara, Filipino-Spanish footballer (b. 1896)
- February 18 – Joseph-Armand Bombardier, Canadian inventor of the snowmobile and founder of Bombardier Inc. (b. 1907)
-

- February 25
  - Johnny Burke, American lyricist (b. 1908)
  - Maurice Farman, French aircraft designer (b. 1877)
  - Grace Metalious, American writer (b. 1924)
- February 26 – F. F. E. Yeo-Thomas, English World War II hero (b. 1901)
- February 27 – Orry-Kelly, Australian-born costume designer (b. 1897)
- February 29 – Frank Albertson, American actor (b. 1909)

March

Paul of Greece

Sigfrid Edstrom

- March 1 – Davíð Stefánsson, Icelandic poet (b. 1895)
- March 4 – Edwin August, American actor and director (b. 1883)

- March 6
  - Paul of Greece, King of Greece (b. 1901)
  - Edward Van Sloan, American actor (b. 1882)
- March 9 – Paul von Lettow-Vorbeck, German general (b. 1870)
- March 13 – Friedrich Lahrs, German architect (b. 1880)
- March 18
  - Sigfrid Edström, Swedish president of the International Olympic Committee (b. 1870)
  - Norbert Wiener, American mathematician (b. 1894)
- March 20 – Brendan Behan, Irish poet and writer (b. 1923)
- March 22 – Addison Richards, American actor (b. 1887)
- March 23 – Peter Lorre, Hungarian-born actor (b. 1904)

April

Douglas MacArthur

- April 5 – Douglas MacArthur, U.S. Army general, Supreme Allied Commander in Japan after World War II (b. 1880)
- April 13 – Veit Harlan, German film director (b. 1899)
- April 14 – Rachel Carson, American biologist and environmental writer (b. 1907)
- April 18 – Ben Hecht, American screenwriter (b. 1894)

- April 20 – Joseph-Alphida Crete, Canadian Politician (b. 1890)
- April 24 – Gerhard Domagk, German bacteriologist, recipient of the Nobel Prize in Physiology or Medicine (declined) (b. 1895)
- April 26 – E. J. Pratt, Canadian poet (b. 1882)
- April 29 – J. M. Kerrigan, Irish actor (b. 1884)

May

Jawaharlal Nehru

Leó Szilárd

- May 2 – Nancy Astor, Viscountess Astor, American-born politician (b. 1879)
- May 10 – Carol Haney, American dancer and actress (b. 1924)
- May 13 – Diana Wynyard, English actress (b. 1906)
- May 17 – Steve Owen, American football coach (New York Giants) and a member of the Pro Football Hall of Fame (b. 1898)
- May 21 – James Franck, German-born physicist, Nobel Prize laureate (b. 1882)
- May 27 – Jawaharlal Nehru, Prime Minister of India (b. 1889)
-

- May 30
  - Dave MacDonald, sports car driver (b. 1936)
  - Eddie Sachs, auto racing driver (b. 1927)
  - Leó Szilárd, Hungarian-American physicist (b. 1898)

June

- June 3 – Frans Eemil Sillanpää, Finnish writer, Nobel Prize laureate (b. 1888)
- June 6 – Robert Warwick, American actor (b. 1878)
- June 7
  - Violet Attlee, Countess Attlee, wife of former British PM Clement Attlee (b. 1895)
  - Charlie Llewellyn, first non-white South African Test cricketer (b. 1876)
- June 9 – Max Aitken, 1st Baron Beaverbrook, Canadian-born newspaper publisher and politician (b. 1879)
- June 11 – Plaek Phibunsongkhram, Thai field marshal, prime minister, and dictator (b. 1897)
- June 17 – Clarence G. Badger, American film director (b. 1880)
- June 21
  - James Chaney, African-American civil rights activist (killed in Mississippi) (b. 1943)
  - Andrew Goodman, American civil rights activist (killed in Mississippi) (b. 1943)
  - Michael Schwerner, American civil rights activist (killed in Mississippi) (b. 1939)
- June 25 – Gerrit Rietveld, Dutch architect (b. 1888)
- June 27 – Mona Barrie, English actress (b. 1909)

July

- July 1 – Pierre Monteux, French conductor (b. 1875)
- July 2 – Glenn "Fireball" Roberts, American race car driver and a member of the NASCAR Hall of Fame (b. 1929)
- July 4 – Hank Sylvern, U.S. radio personality (b. 1908)
- July 6 – Zeng Junchen, Sichuan's 'King of Opium'
- July 7 – Lillian Copeland, American athlete (b. 1904)
- July 13 – Stephen Galatti, Director of AFS, American Field Service (b. 1888)
- July 16 – Alfred Junge, German-born art director (b. 1886)
- July 23 – Thakin Kodaw Hmaing, Burmese poet and politician (b. 1876)
- July 26 – William A. Seiter, American film director (b. 1890)
- July 29 – Vean Gregg, American baseball player (b. 1885)
- July 31 – Jim Reeves, American country singer (b. 1923)

August

Aleksander Zawadzki

Gracie Allen

- August – Salima Machamba Sultan of Mohéli (b. 1874)
- August 3 – Flannery O'Connor, American writer (b. 1925)
- August 6 – Sir Cedric Hardwicke, English actor (b. 1893)
- August 7 – Aleksander Zawadzki, former President of Poland (b. 1899)
- August 9 – Fontaine Fox, American cartoonist (b. 1884)
- August 12
  - Ian Fleming, British writer (b. 1908)
  - Ernst Kühnel, German art historian (b. 1882)
  - Dmitry Dmitrievich Maksutov, Russian astronomer and inventor (b. 1896)
- August 21 – Palmiro Togliatti, Italian communist leader (b. 1893)
- August 27 – Gracie Allen, American actress and comedian (*Burns And Allen*) (b. 1895)

September

- September 2
  - Glenn Albert Black, American archaeologist (b. 1900)
  - Francisco Craveiro Lopes, 12nd President of Portugal (b. 1894)
  - Alvin Cullum York, American hero of World War I (b. 1887)
- September 18
  - Clive Bell, English art critic (b. 1881)
  - Seán O'Casey, Irish writer (b. 1880)
- September 23 – Fred M. Wilcox, American motion picture director (b. 1907)
- September 28
  - Nacio Herb Brown, American songwriter (b. 1896)

- Harpo Marx, American comedian (*Marx Brothers*) (b. 1888)

October

Herbert Hoover

- October 10 – Eddie Cantor, American actor, comedian and dancer (b. 1892)
- October 15 – Cole Porter, American composer (*You're The Top*) (b. 1891)
- October 20 – Herbert Hoover, 31st President of the United States (b. 1874)
- October 22 – Whip Wilson, American actor (b. 1911)
- October 26 – Eric Edgar Cooke, Australian serial killer (b. 1931)
- October 27
  - Pierre Cartier, French jeweller (b. 1878)
  - Rudolph Maté, Polish cinematographer (b. 1898)

November

- November 2 – Charles Walter Allfrey, British general (b. 1895)
- November 5
  - Mabel Lucie Attwell, British illustrator (b. 1879)

- ○ John S. Robertson, Canadian film director (b. 1878)
- November 6 – Hans von Euler-Chelpin, German-born chemist, Nobel Prize laureate (b. 1873)
- November 10 – Jimmie Dodd, American actor and TV personality (b. 1910)
- November 14 – Heinrich von Brentano, German politician (b. 1904)
- November 25 – Clarence Kolb, American actor (b. 1874)
- November 29 – Anne de Vries, Dutch writer (b. 1904)

December

Victor Francis Hess

- December 1 – J. B. S. Haldane, British geneticist (b. 1892)
- December 3 – Charles P. Snyder, American admiral (b. 1879)
- December 5 – V. Veerasingam, Ceylon Tamil teacher and politician (b. 1892)
- December 6 – Consuelo Vanderbilt, Duchess of Marlborough (b. 1877)
- December 9 – Dame Edith Sitwell, British poet (b. 1887)
- December 11
    - ○ Sam Cooke – African-American singer and songwriter (b. 1931)
    - ○ Percy Kilbride, American actor (b. 1888)

- o Alma Schindler Mahler, wife of Gustav Mahler (b. 1879)
- December 14
  - o William Bendix, American actor (b. 1906)
  - o Francisco Canaro, Uruguayan-born composer (b. 1888)
- December 17 – Victor Francis Hess, Austrian-born physicist, Nobel Prize laureate (b. 1883)
- December 21 – Carl Van Vechten, American writer and photographer (b. 1880)
- December 28 – Cliff Sterrett, American cartoonist (b. 1883)
- December 29 – Vladimir Favorsky, Russian artist and engraver (b. 1886)
- December 31
  - o Gertrude Michael, American actress (b. 1911)
  - o Ólafur Thors, Prime Minister of Iceland (b. 1892)
  - o Henry Maitland Wilson, British field marshal (b. 1881)

Date unknown

- Adolfo Díaz Recinos, former President of Nicaragua (b. 1875)

Nobel Prizes

- Physics – Charles Hard Townes, Nicolay Gennadiyevich Basov, Aleksandr Prokhorov
- Chemistry – Dorothy Crowfoot Hodgkin
- Physiology or Medicine – Konrad Bloch, Feodor Lynen
- Literature – Jean-Paul Sartre
- Peace – Martin Luther King Jr.

In the News

The abolition of the death penalty in UK.

President Lyndon Johnson declares a War On Poverty Campaign.

Cassius Clay Beats Sonny Liston on February 25th for World Heavyweight championship.

The most powerful earthquake in U.S. history at a magnitude of 9.2, strikes South Central Alaska.

Nelson Mandela and seven others are sentenced on June 12th to life imprisonment in South Africa.

Elizabeth Taylor marries Richard Burton for the first time.

James Hoffa is found guilty and sentenced to eight years on bribery charges.

U.S. Surgeon General reports that smoking may lead to lung cancer.

Great Train Robbers get 30 years each.

Jack Ruby is convicted of the murder of Lee Harvey Oswald, the alleged assassin of President Kennedy

Popular Films - The Carpetbaggers, It's a Mad, Mad, Mad, Mad World, The Unsinkable Molly Brown, My Fair Lady, Mary Poppins.

www.ingramcontent.com/pod-product-compliance
Lightning Source LLC
Chambersburg PA
CBHW060207290526
45789CB00003B/1197